I0671108

Notes from the Girl in Seat 7

Notes from the Girl in Seat 7

By
A.E. Grove

Illustrations by
Robyn Ryan

Wallace Press

Wallace Press — seatseven@gmail.com
Oak Grove, VA

ISBN 978-0-6151-5644-6

Illustrations by Robyn Ryan
Ballyryan Studios, P.O. Box 865, Fredericksburg, VA 22404
rryan@hughes.net   www.absolutearts.com/robynryan

Cover Art and Design by Daniel Wallace

Description: An anthology of poetry and short stories covering a
wide range of topics from nature to fantasy to ethics.

Acknowledgements

I would like to acknowledge my teacher, friend, and mentor, Jane Grimes, and to let her know my profound appreciation for her guidance through the years.

I would also like to express gratitude toward my parents, for supplying the cover photographs, and for always encouraging me and building me up.

Finally, I must offer many thanks to Robyn Ryan, for the insightful illustrations which have reflected much of the essence of these poems and stories, and have helped make this book what it is.

Dedication

… see page 4!

Notes from the Girl in Seat 7

Table of Contents

Preface

On my school bus, the one I have ridden to and from school since I was in the sixth grade, the seats are numbered. All the odd-numbered seats are on the right; the even ones, the left. I sit on the right-hand side, in seat seven.

That's the origin of much of this book.

The ride to school is long—roughly an hour from my house by bus. When I first rode that route, I used to hate it... until it taught me something.

That ride, at first an inconvenient burden, soon became my sanctuary. When I would board in the morning, much of the world (including those around me) slept. The sun slept, too, and much of my work I wrote by its first rays.

My thoughts were left to themselves.

Slowly but certainly, I came to find that this small, private world within the range of a single bus seat could come alive. I sometimes wonder if perhaps the stories and poems were actually on the bus to begin with, waiting for me to join them and free them. And while several of these works were written away from the bus, it seems the ideas have planted their seeds inside my hands, to write more as I am away from the source. Who knows?

I know this, though. The years that have passed since I first boarded that bus have spun many tales and poems of their own. A few of these can be found in this book.

Now they're yours.

Gratitude

Believe it or not…

I pity those who
    Don't need glasses
    For they don't know
  What the world looks like
    Without them:

  They don't know the way
  Tree leaves melt together
Into smooth, rippling ponds
    Of green
  They don't know the way
A bed or a couch goes soft
Before your eyes, in a pool
    Of comfort
  They don't know the way
  Street lamps burst out
  Bearing the images
    Of lions' manes

I pity those who
    Don't need braces
    For they don't know
  The sweetness of food
    Without them:

  They don't know the way
  Popcorn's flavor lingers
When one must eat slowly
    And carefully
  They don't know the way
A peanut warms the mouth
  When eaten one by one
    And one only
  They don't know the way
  Gum is extra chewy
After two years of waiting
    And waiting

I pity those who
    Don't need school buses
    For they don't know
  What they are missing
    Without one:

  They don't know the way
  An hour-long route
    Gives one time
    To think
  They don't know the way
  The crisp morning light
  Sends one the vision
    To reflect
  They don't know the way
  One has a sanctuary,
  A block of time
    To write

I pity those who
Pity me
For they don't know:
      I have the things
      I need

Because I Can Speak

The crystal was in the woods
When he found it
It shone
It shone neither Black nor
White
It shone both White and
Black
Dispel the notion it shone gray
It shone and did not shine Black and White
But as he looked at it
And refused to ponder the Black
It shone White
Because he couldn't see
The Black

He brought it to his village
Where the people commenced
The argument
The debate
The controversy
A White stone should be let in
A Black stone should be kept out
These they had been taught since the cradle
Everyone knew them
Even the children
Even the outcasts
Even the foreigners
But was this a White stone
Or a Black stone?

He saw it as White
So he brought the stone in
Without considering
Did the White outweigh the Black?

Once the crystal came
The Things happened
The village knew of Things
When a new stone was brought in
Things always happened
Good Things. Bad Things.
Things had to happen…
It was the meaning of crystals!

And once it was in
Those who could speak were healed
And rejoiced
Those who could not speak perished
And could not scream their pain
All reports were positive
All testimonies joyful
For those who had suffered and were slain
Could not be witnesses
The village cheered in glorious
Celebration
Of their sacred White stone

But I warn you, reader,
You are a living villager, as am I,
And you and I must both testify
That all along
The stone was
Black

Ode to All Parents of Any Children Who Have Withstood Peer Pressure

I sit and sit and I sit more
Along this room's wood paneled floor
I struggle till my brain is sore
To think what I've been taught before
Rememb'ring guidance, less or more
Of instructions, which implore
I must hold strong to plain sense, or
I'll soon slip through a dang'rous door

A PA system sounds off clear
These words I am forbade to hear
Forbade or not, for all that's dear,
I stay, for one can't exit here!
I look around, and every peer
Listens freely, without fear
Since I do not, they think me queer
"Non-list'ners" strange to them appear

And now hypnosis works its way
Trav'ling through the room's PA
Slowly melting far away
Are minds surrounding me today
I've been taught, "Don't fall astray."
I filter through the things they say
And from their drumbeat turn away
My mind is mine, and mine to stay

Their heads possessed, and thoughts askew,
They act as I would never do
Poisons they commence to chew
They break what they cannot renew
Chaos and disorder brew
As brains are stripped of all they knew
The hypnotized cannot construe
Refusal of succumbing too

But as I stand and as I see
The victims fall in front of me
I recall a heartfelt plea
Of those who have looked out for me
Who told me how the Earth should be
Whose instructions set me free
Even if they weren't with me
They warned of voices I should flee

Now I say, "Thank you."

The Autumn

Geese flying south,
Apples in my mouth,
Leaves dancing off the trees,
Frost is biting at my knees!

Cranberries, turkey, pie to munch,
Are part of my Thanksgiving lunch
Costumes, candy, trick-or-treat,
Halloween is hard to beat!

The sky, the animals, and trees too,
All agree, and you may too,
That the most wonderful season of all
Is certainly, certainly,
The season of fall!

Starlight

The universe must stop somewhere
So there is a point
Where all the galaxies
end
Where there is no
life
Where it is incredibly
cold
Beyond everything
Where the whole universe
is just a speck
in the distance

Yet what if way out there
Googols of light-years away
Beyond the nebulas'
clouds
Beyond the hoards
of stars
Beyond the spinning
solar systems
Somehow, way out there
Is a singular,
on its own
solitary star

This isolated, far-away star,
Abandoned by our universe,
Has no other
stars
Has not a single
planet
Has not even an
asteroid
To call its very own
There's nothing, absolutely
nothing else
at all

But somehow, it keeps shining
Although it may never be seen
No one cares for
it
No one feels its
warmth
No one will even
see it
Something keeps it going
Although we're all preoccupied
with bigger,
brighter stars

Why does it continue to shine?
After all, nobody notices it,
Surpassed by bigger
stars
Surpassed by stars of
more beauty
Surpassed by closer stars
to Earth
Why does it shine?
Because it is a star
and it does what
it was meant to do

Notes from the Girl in Seat 7

Joined

"Hide me, Sylvie."

It sounded so strange, having my best friend come to the door to request that. I mean, normally when Samantha came to my house, it was regarding a cute football player who never noticed her, or a killer math test, or a CD she wanted to show me. She never asked me to hide her.

"Ha, ha," I responded. "What is it now? Aunt Margarite?" Aunt Margarite was Samantha's dad's sister. She was maybe thirteen years older than Samantha's dad, who wasn't a spring chicken himself. She always took Samantha's room, making her sleep on the couch, and expected Samantha to wear dresses to school and call everyone who was older "ma'am" and "sir", even if the difference was only three years. She visited twice a year, during which Samantha would escape to my house as often as possible.

"No," she said, gasping. Odd. She doesn't gasp. She's on the cross-country team, and can run for miles without really needing to breathe. "Listen. Hide me first. Then I'll explain."

"*Hide* you?"

"Yes," she said, as though it wasn't an odd request at all. "In the most secretive place you can."

I thought a moment, not about where to hide her but of the request. Why did she need to be hidden? I racked my brain for possible reasons but came up with nothing. Was a psycho stalking her on the street? No, then she would ask me to call 911 before hiding her. Was this some stupid hide-and-seek game? Again, no. She looked too serious.

Noting her panicked expression, I told her, "Of course you can hide here. Under the eaves in my room." After all, she was my best friend. And in my room, there is a tiny closet that only we know about. My parents really didn't inspect the room much when they bought the house when I was eight. Or maybe they did. I didn't actually notice the little, almost invisible door until nearly a year after we moved in. Since then, Samantha and I had spent many afternoons playing in that miniscule attic-like closet, never telling anyone about it. We stored stuff in there we wanted to keep secret, such as candy, which we'd use to stuff ourselves silly and didn't want the grown-ups

11

confiscating, or photos of hot movie stars, or toys we were "too old" for.

She ran up the stairs after me. I dashed into my room, pushed my little brother out, and locked the door behind us. She opened the closet door and slipped in, with me following. It was something of a tight squeeze, since we'd sort of fallen out of the habit of going in there when we were about twelve.

Inside, it was somehow smaller than I remembered. With the two of us, plus the crate of junk from our childhood and a pile of tangly-haired Barbies, there really wasn't room for anything else.

"Okay, you're hidden. Now tell me why," I told her, once we were situated.

"I'm... running," she muttered.

"Running? From whom?"

"Myself."

I stared at her.

"Yourself?"

She nodded. "I know. It's strange. But let me explain."

"Have you done something?"

She shook her head, then stopped abruptly.

"Well, I did do something. But not this me. The other me's. Now there's only one."

I was completely confused.

"Look," she said. "Don't try to understand immediately. Try to listen. Then it will all make sense."

She took a deep breath and began.

"First off, there isn't just one me. There are many of me, stretched across time and space."

"Like reincarnation?"

"No. It's not the same me in a new body. It can't be, because sometimes there are two or more in the world at one time, just in different cultures. Also, it's the same kind of body every time... well, mostly. Like, I don't go back and forth from species to species, or even from gender to gender."

"How do you know this?"

"'I' told myself. I don't know how, but a couple weeks ago another one of me came here and now. Like time traveled or something."

I still felt puzzled. Yet, stupid as the story was, and disinclined as I was to believe it, somehow I found myself believing every word.

"And anyway, even though the bodies are different, a few things are remarkably the same. Like how every one of 'me' was five years old when she lost her first tooth. Or how we... me... whatever... all broke our left arm by falling at age nine and a half. Stuff like that."

"That's strange. I'm sorry, but I--"

"I know, I know. But listen. That's not what's important. The thing is, my other selves have found a way of... joining up. As in, through time travel or whatever it is, the other selves have met up and meshed their bodies together. As in, two people have formed into one person. And they all did it at the point in time when each of them was sixteen. But I didn't want to join them."

"Why not?"

"Because as the girls join up, the body gets stronger. And smarter. Basically, two people in one. Then three. Then four. When I was asked to join, I somehow wasn't sure I wanted to. So they... I... she... gave me more time. The other selves also asked to wait before they Joined, which made this seem like just another likeness. And during that time, I did some research on the names of my other selves. And do you know what? That power must have been corrupting. In looking at biographies of myself, I found horrible things. Things like where 'I' tricked kings out of their kingdoms. Things like where 'I' set fire to whole cities. Things like where 'I' murdered people. But if this is really me, and I would never do that, it must have been something to do with the group effort. It must, because none of it happened before 'I' was sixteen. I mean... I'm not that bad, am I?"

I stared at her. "Of course not! You wouldn't!"

"Exactly. And I don't want to be part of someone who would, at any rate. But... 'I've' come back. And when I refused, 'I' tried to make me Join. The other 'I' said it was simply the way things had to be, because we were all the same. So I... the real I... ran away. Now please, will you keep me here?"

I nodded. She was my friend. And I... thought I believed her.

"What makes you think that will work?"

I looked up to the sound of her voice.

Then realized my friend hadn't said anything.

Turning my head, I saw that there, in the door to my closet, stood Samantha.

13

I rubbed my eyes. I was seeing double. Two Samanthas. One kneeling on the closet floor in front of me, gasping in fear. The other standing threateningly in the doorway of my closet.

It did prove one thing, though: Samantha was right. Insane as her story was, it was true.

"Come. You must join," Doorway Samantha said, yanking Closet Samantha out of the closet. Yet as I looked at DS, I realized that though her features were remarkably similar to CS, she still didn't look entirely the same. Sure, it was the same height, posture, face shape, and hair texture, but some things were still radically different. DS was quite dark skinned, with narrow, Oriental eyes and flamboyant red hair. She looked very strange. Maybe that was what happened when Samanthas of different genetic backgrounds suddenly became one Samantha.

I followed them out of the closet, my heart beating wildly.

"But of course, a Joining cannot have witnesses," DS told CS. Then she turned fierce. "You told her everything, didn't you?"

"No! I--"

"You cannot lie to me. Don't you know? Every human on the planet has a very slight ability to distinguish truth from falsehoods. Yet it is such a miniscule power it seldom does anyone good. But with a Joining..." She sneered. "With a Joining, the power increases. There are so many contained within this one body that I cannot be lied to now. You did tell her everything. Join me. But first we must have no witnesses."

She laughed and pointed to me. The next thing I knew, a strange, electric-blue hourglass hung around my neck.

"I am not so horrid. You must die. Even if you did not see, you know too much. However, I will let you live long enough to see the Joining. It really is beautiful..."

"How... how did you do that?" I sputtered.

"Like discernment of truth, it's another power one gains slowly as more people Join. There are many of me, thousands, here. And with each new one, my power grows just a tiny bit. Power," she said, looking at CS, "that will soon be yours."

"And what if I don't want to Join?" my best friend shot back.

"Don't be a fool. I can force you to Join. I forced many of myselves into the rest. They didn't want to, either. But even so... don't you *want* to Join?"

"And be like you? No way!"

"Fool. You will never be complete until you Join. There will be one part of you here, and the rest floating through time and places. Don't you see? You are not whole. Don't you want the all of you to be together? You are the last one we need to Join. Then we can see what happens when one's whole self is together. I do not know... won't it be wonderful?"

There was a strange look on her face. It wasn't manipulation, or anger, or sheer threat. It was... pleading. As if this was what she truly wanted. As if this big, powerful creature were thirsty and being denied a drink. My friend, however, was not sucked in.

"And be like you? You've done terrible things. I can't be you."

"That was all necessary. I had to use my power, to take control, if I was ever to find those who would make me whole. My other selves. And now... when we take you, we will finally *all* be here."

"Then what? If you would stoop to such levels, just to collect these pieces, what would we do when we were together? You're killing my best friend! I can't trust you. I don't want all your... pieces. Pieces I could live without. I am happy now, in my own world, in my own time. Perhaps it was only with Joining that you began to feel hollow, and then you collected more. When we're all together, it will be not the fullest, but the emptiest and darkest existence we will have. I'm not Joining!"

She started for the door, but was held back as if by an unseen force. DS, who was very strong in all her power, had seized her.

"You cannot escape. The rest of us Joined when we were sixteen. You have to... you're one of us!"

"I won't!" she screamed, then snatched my hourglass.

The sand was very low.

"Samantha," I sobbed. I hadn't realized I was crying. "Samantha, you can't save..."

"*I* have to die," she said. She put it around her neck.

"No!" DS's eyes widened in horror.

The last grain fell through.

An enormous blue light filled my room, and all Samanthas shrieked, in a chorus of many voices.

All of them?

All the Samanthas lay in my room, barely breathing. There were thousands, but somehow they all fit. They all looked different. There were Egyptian Samanthas, Romans, Aztecs, Greeks, Indians, Chinese, Israelites, and many I didn't have a clue about.

What was happening?

Then I understood. They could no longer be Joined.

Because there was a break in the chain.

I realized all of a sudden that, considering how long Samantha spent gathering herself, the original would no longer be sixteen now, but would be seventeen, eighteen, nineteen... who knew?

But the Samantha I knew died at sixteen.

She was no longer one of them. Yet because she had been a part of the web, the others could no longer be Joined to each other.

"Thank you," the others whispered. "For delivering us from our own darkness."

Almost in unison, their last breaths escaped their lips.

Then they disappeared.

Of course, I thought. *So much of what they did, they did together. Now they could not have.* Meaning... they couldn't have existed. Could they?

No, they couldn't have. I knew that as I gazed around the room.

I'm still watching. Watching as, one by one, memoirs of my best friend leave my room. The trophy we won when we entered an art contest together. The photograph of us at our middle school "graduation." The sweater she gave me for Christmas.

She no longer exists. She no longer existed. She no longer will exist.

As every trace of the friend who saved my life, who saved history, leaves the room, a sad thought fills my head.

The last thing to clear will be my mind.

Your Conscience

Inside of everybody
There dwells a little man
He's aware of what you do
As often as he can

He feels it when you're sassy
And that you told a lie
And took your sister's candy
Poked your brother in the eye

He yells when you're not doing right
He shouts when you do wrong
But his cries grow far less loud
When you do it very long

The first shout -- it should teach you
To not repeat your crime
But if you do, he's not as loud
Upon the second time

His voice will get much fainter
The more you sin around
Until, finally, sad to say,
You will not hear a sound

As you read this tragic tale,
Keep in mind, of course,
The moral of the story here:
Don't let this guy get hoarse

The Stones of Time

The opal gleam of sunrise
The topaz when it sets
The turquoise blue of middle-day
The onyx black night gets

The jade grass blooms in summer's life
The ruby apples autumn makes
The sapphire ice in winter's cold
Spring pearl lilies on the lakes

A windy day has agate swirls
A snowy day is diamond white
Aquamarine on rainy days
Bloodstone zips through stormy night

Through any type of weather
Through work or play or school
Through any time of day or year
Each moment is a jewel

Notes from the Girl in Seat 7

Patience
a Tanka

A morning glory-
I am one of those flowers
But now I'm closed tight
In waiting for the morning
Holding my beauty inside

Other flowers near
Open, though there is no light
They love their beauty
And see no reason to wait
To display it for the world

But moonlight is weak
Their beauty is not well seen
For there's no sunlight
And when the dawn will arrive
They shrivel, with no beauty

They mock me right now
For their beauty is open
But mine is closed, yet
This morning glory waits, and
Will be lovely, with sunlight

The Garden of Sunlight

Once upon a time, in a forest far away, there was a garden. It was at the center of the forest, between every village, and its soil was the most fertile throughout the wood. Many lovely flowers grew there. Nearly all the villagers tended it. They began at different ages—sometimes as young as thirteen, sometimes as old as thirty, sometimes even older. But most came to the Garden eventually. And once they started to tend it, they would help care for it beautifully for the rest of their lives.

Every day it was a lovely ceremony. It started with the ringing of bells in the Garden. Then the women came out in fine gowns of white silk, and the people promptly set about the care of their thousands of flowers, as a loving sun bestowed its blessed rays upon the plants below.

Until one day.

A young man of maybe sixteen came forth. He said, "You know, I do not believe I was ever meant for this Garden." He looked upon the Garden powerfully with disdain in his eye. Then he walked away.

He came across a mud puddle. It was nothing like the gorgeous fountain that watered the Garden's plants. But he told himself, *This is what I was meant for.* He repeated it until he believed it.

So for days afterward, he strained and struggled to yield flowers of his very own. When he could not, he picked up a withered stalk and presented it to the other villagers. "See," he told them, "I can produce things of beauty in *my* garden."

"But, sir," an older man asked, "it is not a flower, or a tree, or a vine. It is merely a single stalk!"

"To the closed-minded, yes," the boy responded. "You see it as a stalk. But I see a gorgeous plant worthy of cultivation."

Excited whispers flowed among the crowd.

"Excuse me," a girl stated, "but I believe I was meant for your flowers as well. The gardening I have attempted does not work for me."

"You are young. Give it time. Your section of the Garden will blossom someday," a middle-aged woman told them.

"Or will it?" a man responded. "Some people are born to garden flowers in the main Garden. Others may have been meant to tend other gardens. Can't we just accept the way we were born?"

"But you *chose* to use the mud hole."

"We did not choose it. It is how we were born. When did *you* make the 'decision' to use *your* Garden?"

"Our Garden has the sun. Yours is in the shade. How can it grow? It never gets any sunlight!"

"Which is why I don't believe in the sun," another woman replied. "Why would such a warm and loving sun not shine on our garden just because it's different?"

The argument continued. Soon many villagers left to tend the stalks and thorny vines by the mud. Once in a while, someone would try to talk them back into using the Garden. But these attempts were always refused, and their deliverers were shunned for not accepting all ways of doing things.

Gradually, over the years, more and more people left the security of the Garden and attempted to garden by the puddle, expressing love for it yet neglecting their own plants. Soon they desperately gave up on gardening at all.

Those who kept the Garden often tried to handle the work by themselves, but they could not. Soon, the place became overgrown with weeds, the fountain's motor ran down, and the benches became rusty with age.

But the sun still loved it warmly, as always.

Notes from the Girl in Seat 7

The Messenger

Once upon a time, a man and a woman lived together happily in their house in a quiet, countryside village. One day, however, the man fell very ill and his wife, understanding he could die, called for a doctor. A few minutes later, someone knocked on the door.

"I'm a doctor," he called. "Please let me in."

The wife, overjoyed that her sick husband would be taken care of, answered the door.

The doctor entered. He told the couple, "This man must be cured with this ointment." And he pulled out a little green tube and smeared it all over the man's face, chest, and arms. With that, the doctor departed.

No sooner had he left than the woman noticed an odd smell about her husband. It was very minty and strong, and she found it rather overwhelming. Suddenly, a thought dawned on her. She scraped a little ointment off the man's face and ran upstairs. She came back down minutes later, her face appearing very angry.

"Husband!" she exclaimed. "That doctor tricked us! All he did was smear ordinary toothpaste over you!"

And with that, she called for another doctor.

A few minutes later, somebody else knocked. "I'm a doctor," he called. "Please let me in."

The wife ran to the door, pleased that she had gotten hold of a proper doctor to cure her husband.

This doctor came in. He said, "To get well, you must get exercise. Run outside and bring me twelve eggs from the hen house."

"But sir, my husband is so weak he can scarcely stand!"

"Then he is going to die." The doctor started to leave. The wife stopped him.

"My husband will bring you the eggs!"

So the man weakly stumbled toward the hen house. Once he got back, the doctor said, "Very good. Now, for more exercise, fetch a bucket of water and bring it to me."

"But he can't! My husband is still very tired from retrieving the eggs!"

"Then he is going to die."

And so it went for much of the afternoon, until, after carrying an enormous load of logs, the poor man collapsed on the floor.

"I'm sorry, doctor," the wife stated, "but we cannot continue this cure any longer. Look at my husband!"

"Then he will have to die." The doctor left.

"You know, wife," the man mumbled as he came to, "I don't think that doctor was very helpful either." He passed out again.

The wife called once more for another doctor. A while later, there was a knock at the door.

"I'm a doctor," he called. "Please let me in."

The wife, desperate that *somebody* could cure her husband, opened the door.

The doctor slipped inside. He pulled several bottles out of his bag. "Take any one you like. Pick whatever you think works."

"Whatever *I* think works?" the man asked.

"Yes," the doctor answered. "I shouldn't recommend one over the other. It would be arrogant of me to suggest that *one* might be the only cure. I will tolerantly accept your choice, no matter what it may or may not be."

Nervously, the man reached for a bottle. He started to drink, but it tasted horrible. He tried a second one, but it burned as he swallowed it. He tried a third and a fourth, which, respectively, smelled horrible and gave him terrible nausea. He gave up after looking over the vast array of offerings.

"I... don't think any of them would work for me..." he muttered.

"So you have chosen to heal without medicine. To get better on your own strength. That is okay. I'm open-minded."

"So what was the point of coming in the first place?" the woman snapped. She shooed away this last incompetent doctor.

A last knock came at the door.

"I'm The Doctor," He called. "Please let Me in."

"No!" screamed the woman. "Doctors don't really do anything! I'm never calling one again!"

"But I can save your—"

"Sure, save him just like the others did! Go away!"

Sighing, the Doctor turned and walked away, His medicine at His side, mourning the man He would have saved.

Notes from the Girl in Seat 7

Focus

The skilled Gardener
Loved His plants
He loved His flowers
His trees
His bushes
His shrubs
His vines
And daily He watered them
And weeded them
And cared for them
The garden was all His own work
And as it was His, He loved it
The vast rows far beyond the realm of vision
The intricate latticework beside the shed
Was all His doing

Then He reached down
And watered a single daisy
For she was of His garden too

Optimism
a Haiku

The grass is greener
On the other side of the
Fence, or so I'm told

Yet if you look up
You will find a sky that is
Bluest where you stand

Cooperation

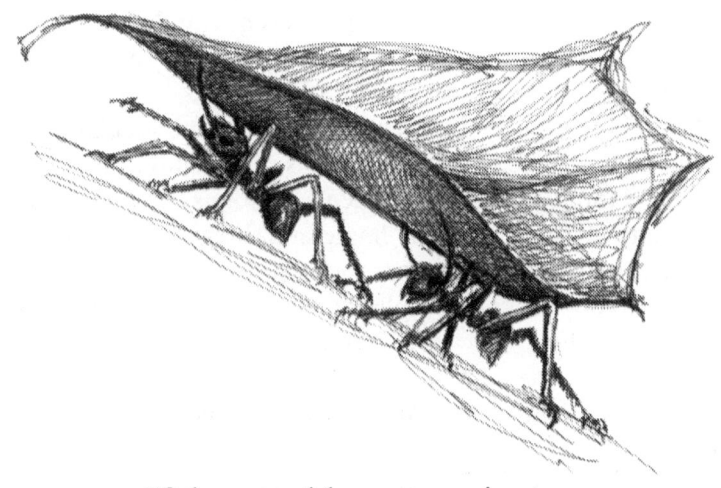

If time could spare a minute
And our world and people in it
And all and each one's brother
Worked along with one another,

Then the things that we could do
And the thoughts we could construe
Would cover vast a ground
For here is what I found:

Six billion in
One minute's frame
Could make results
Which are the same
As much as one
If he began
With the very
Dawn of man

Mere Luck

I opened the wrapper of a piece of chewing gum and placed the stick inside my mouth. My ears have always felt uncomfortable when planes take off or land, but chewing gum has always helped. As the plane approached the landing strip below, my tongue slowly absorbed the fresh, minty flavor.

My first thought as I stepped off of the plane was how lucky I was. I was sixteen, a good student, and, as of the start of the school year in one week, a foreign exchange student. I had just flown into the American state of Texas from my homeland, Ireland. I would be staying with a family there, the Perkinses.

I pulled out the photograph they had sent. The family had nine children. Nine! There were three boys, named Philip, Lars, and Enrique. The six girls were named Cecilia, Liz-Bette, Cynthia, Miriam, Lynne, and Josephina. *With all those children already,* I wondered, *why on Earth are they taking in a foreign exchange student?*

Yet as I peered at the photo, a strange thought crept into my mind: This family did not look very much alike. The mother was short and had long, wavy red hair that reached her waste. The father was tall, extremely bony, and had a black mustache and square glasses. The children, however, bore little resemblance to their parents or to each other. There were children who could have played basketball and children who, if they were any smaller, would not have been there at all. Some kids had freckles, while others had fair skin. There was brown hair, blonde hair, and black hair, as well as blue eyes, brown eyes, green eyes, and, on one child (Cecilia), eyes that were mismatched between hazel and blue. And they looked close in age-- the youngest couldn't have been less than fourteen, while the oldest looked no more than nineteen.

I wonder if some of them are adopted, I thought. Out of politeness, I decided not to ask until I was closer to the family.

The plane landed and I got off at the airport in Houston. Sure enough, Mr. Perkins was waiting for me, looking exactly like he did in the picture. Upon closer examination, I realized he was even wearing the same outfit.

"Hello, Mr. Perkins," I greeted him.

"Hello, Peter. Pleased to meet you in person. I'm sorry the rest of my family couldn't come, but my wife was so worried about a clean house and everything that she put herself and the children to work. Now, are you hungry? It's about noon, so you must want some lunch..."

I looked at my watch. Noon? It had been long since noon. Then I realized.

"Mr. Perkins, I ate before I left. I ate in a different time zone, remember?" Right then and there, I adjusted my watch to display the correct time.

"Oh... of course," he muttered. "Well, then I guess we can just hit the road, then, as soon as you have your luggage and passport checked and everything."

Soon we were on our way to the small town of San Jorge. We passed what was to be my new high school, Blue Fern High, and I felt a shiver of excitement.

About two hours after we had left the airport, the car stopped in, of all places, the parking lot of a funeral home. My mind raced with questions. *Why are we here? Is there a viewing Mr. Perkins was going to stop at? No, that's absurd; he would have told me if there had been a death!*

"Need any help with your luggage?" he asked.

"What-- sir?" I asked, confused.

"Our apartment-- it's right over this building."

"You live *here?*" Suddenly, I clamped my hand over my mouth, shocked at my own rudeness.

Mr. Perkins laughed. "Did I forget to tell you? I'm a mortician. I prepare bodies for burial."

I only nodded and clenched the handle of my suitcase until my knuckles turned snow-white. I had to stay in a place that embalmed dead people?

Sorry, but I have been squeamish my whole life. Death has always been particularly ominous in my family. In fact, my grandmother, who has always been very superstitious and fearful of what she calls "old things," claims that she once had a poltergeist in her room, a mischievous spirit that had misbehaved on earth and was not allowed into heaven but had tricked the devil into not taking his soul. This spirit supposedly had nothing better than to roam the earth making more mischief for all eternity.

But that's how Grandma has always been. I mean, I still can't forget the humiliating time in third grade when Grandma drove me to school. We were early, so I ran around on the playground a little before school started. Some older kids came up and teased me for always having been on the small side. Of course, Grandma came up and told them it's because I have leprechaun in me and that she, as a changeling, had been abandoned by the leprechaun community to be swapped for a human child. I was so embarrassed!

I shrugged and made my way up into the apartment. These people had no idea what my embarrassing childhood moments were, and I hoped to keep it that way!

I wasn't sure what I expected-- a "Welcome, Peter!" banner, a gift on the kitchen table, a bunch of children waiting to greet me? But the house was very silent as I pushed open the door. I could hear sounds of talking coming from the other room, but nobody seemed to be paying any attention to the fact that Mr. Perkins and I had just entered.

I just stared around the apartment. I was standing in a kitchen with pale green wallpaper and a rather old tile floor. Next to it was a tiny living room, from which branched three bedrooms and a bathroom. That was all. The bedrooms were small, too. How on earth did a family of eleven-- twelve, now-- manage in such a miniscule house?

Mrs. Perkins walked in. "Oh, hello, Peter," she greeted me. "Welcome home. I know it doesn't look like much, but we don't spend a lot of time indoors. We go outside a lot, and when we are inside, it's usually downstairs." She pointed to the staircase from which I had just entered my new home.

I became aware, suddenly, that we were not alone. Sure enough, soon a tall, lean girl with dirty-blonde hair came in. I caught sight of her mismatched eyes. This was Cecilia.

"Hello, Peter," she said. She looked about my age and spoke in a quiet, toneless voice. I noticed small bags under each eye, as though she needed more sleep and was not getting it.

Soon the other children came in. They, too, appeared rather weary, and I felt with a pang of guilt that they had probably just spent all day cleaning for me.

Just then, the phone rang. "I'll get it," Mrs. Perkins said. Mr. Perkins went downstairs, leaving me alone with the kids.

"Uh... hi," I said, unsure how to break the ice. "Um, I'm Peter, and I know your names from the picture you sent. It's a very nice photo, by the way."

The kids just shrugged, all nine of them in unison. *They're like robots!* I thought. *They have the same posture, the same gestures, and* (I looked closely, just to be sure) every *one of them is swinging his or her left leg, just a little.*

This was eerie. Clearly they were not talkative sorts. Maybe the stony silence here had to be broken by actions, rather than conversation. "Do you all have any games you like to play?"

"Well," said Enrique, the youngest. "We like to have races in the backyard."

"Yeah," said Josephina, a girl who looked not much older. She was short and skinny, with jet-black hair and big brown eyes. "Want to watch?"

"Sure," I said. To tell the truth, I had never been much one for spectator sports. But I wanted to get through to them, so I pretended to be interested.

We raced down the steps and into the backyard. Enrique, Josephina, and two other kids went inside the shed. Apparently they had go-karts or something they raced.

"So what do you all race?" I asked Philip, a husky, platinum blonde boy who looked maybe seventeen or eighteen.

"Oh, sometimes bikes, sometimes scooters, sometimes roller skates. But mainly we race carts."

"Go-karts?"

"No, just carts. Dad's got some that he uses to move the bodies during embalming."

He looks so natural! I thought. *Like this is* normal!

The four kids returned with two carts, with a couple of children on each. One child would push and another would ride. The afternoon quickly slipped by, with a gentle creaking noise coming from the wheels of the carts. Soon Mr. and Mrs. Perkins called us in for dinner.

"What's for dinner tonight, Mom?" Liz-Bette asked as we tromped up the stairs into the kitchen.

"Oh, I thought we'd celebrate Peter's arrival. I made my special three-nut steak casserole."

The dinner passed pretty much with nothing to report, other than the very odd recipe behind this casserole. I personally rather disliked it (I smelled something very bitter in there somewhere), so rather than eating it I smeared it around to look as though I'd eaten some but had gotten full.

The family began asking questions, things like, "What was your school like in Ireland?" "What about your neighborhood?" and "Do you have any hobbies?" These questions were mainly directed from Mr. and Mrs. Perkins; in fact, come to think of it, I'm not sure I can recall a single word one of the kids said the entire meal.

After dinner, even though it was only a quarter till six, I was exhausted with jet lag. I brushed my teeth, changed into pajamas, and climbed into my room.

When the Perkinses told me which room was mine, I had thought I would be sharing with all the other boys, since the apartment was so miniscule. But Mrs. Perkins had insisted I have my own room. "The children can all share," she had said. "You're our guest."

I almost pointed out that since I would be staying here a year, I was hardly a "guest." But she seemed really intent on giving me my own quarters, so I thanked her and outside to get it.

I was no doubt grateful that I wouldn't be sharing, because the room was hardly big enough for one boy. The bed, which was not a very large one, took up a third of the floor space; the dresser occupied another third. I had no idea how they squeezed three boys inside before, or-- I thought with a dash of guilt-- how they squeezed nine kids into the next room now. I didn't wonder for too long, though. Before I knew it, my drooping eyelids forced me into a warm, deep sleep.

*****

I awoke at three-thirty the next morning. I have always been an early riser, but the time difference made that *really* early. I couldn't get back to sleep, so after a while I decided to just get up.

I was about to get dressed when I remembered: I had left one of my bags in the car. Maybe, without waking anyone, I could tiptoe downstairs and outside to get it.

I opened the kitchen door and crept down the staircase.

I was caught off guard by Mr. Perkins's voice.

At first I thought he was talking in his sleep, but then I realized his voice was coming from the bottom of the steps.

"--and I know my children are quite eager to have a new brother walk amongst them--"

Do they all *get up this early?* I wondered. *And why are they calling me their* brother *all of a sudden? Upstairs, they thought I was a* guest.

The next part sounded really odd:

"Do as I command, and he may join you soon, as soon as tomorrow. I have the fluids ready--"

Tomorrow? I was here *now.* And what fluids?

Lars's voice floated upstairs. "Father, I sense he is awake."

"Do not fret, children. Surely you realize that not one exchange student has yet slipped by me. Eventually you all turn into my slaves."

Run, instinct told me. But where? Upstairs, and I was shut in. Downstairs, and I would walk right into them. I was trapped.

How would I escape? Maybe I could go upstairs, and jump out a window. That might work. I held my breath and tiptoed upstairs.

A low, hissing noise came from behind me. I turned around.

There, with the horrible unison I had witnessed only hours before, the children stood, aligning their steps.

They grew closer.

"Join us," they whispered. "JOIN US!"

I ran. I ran up the stairs to my room, where I had left a window open.

Somehow, it had closed itself again. It wouldn't open or even break.

Closer, closer approached the zombies.

Frantically, I grabbed my suitcase, thrust it open, and searched desperately for something-- anything-- I could use as a weapon. My hands clutched a hard object.

A horseshoe.

The groans stopped.

I looked down at my fist, gripping the iron with dear life.

Grandma. She must have slipped this in for good luck. It was exactly like her to do that.

Thank you, Grandma! I thought, as the wicked throng retreated. I knew that she often told me iron repelled evil. Or maybe it wasn't the iron at all. Maybe it was Grandma.

I watched the Perkinses fall into dust.

Then the house fell too. *Of course.* The Perkinses weren't the only evil ones: the building itself was pure evil. Maybe it was haunted; maybe it simply retained all the wickedness it had held over the years.

I turned and left the ruins. The sound of carts' wheels turning was the last thing I heard as I walked away into the early morning fog.

Lost in Processing

"Do it this way,"
The instructor chants
As we observe her garden
And struggle to make ours
Look like hers

"They must be in rows.
They must be watered
Exactly twice in one day.
There must be precisely four colors,
And twenty-four blossoms in a row."

The others are not gardeners
They see theirs as mere work
Same old, day after day
They see only something needing doing
And have no love for it when it is done

I hate gardening as well
I hate it, for I love it
I love my flowers, in my structure
And when forced to follow a pattern—
It is not *my* garden!

I have a garden— a real garden
But to them it is not one
I have kept mine hidden
And tend it freely
And watch it burst to life

My garden— my rule-breaking garden!
Wrong flowers, wrong colors
In my arrangement of seas,
Vast seas of more than twenty-four
And none of them in rows

My garden is alive
Theirs is dead, but mine lives long
Because it is incorrect,
My instructors do not see it
But they never wanted it anyway

How to Kill Literature

To kill a poem or a story,
Don't burn it—
It's livelier than that
Don't crush it—
It's stronger than that
Don't tear it—
It's tougher than that
To kill a poem or a story,
Dissect it
And pick it apart piece by piece

Make your first cuts
To separate the `exposition`,
The `climax`,
The `resolution`
Then— snip, snip—
Pluck out the sentences
And classify them
Prod and correctly label
The following: `alliteration`,
`Consonance`, `assonance`, `end rhyme`
Find at least two `similes`,
Three `metaphors`, and `personification`
This anatomy must be
Exact, precise, sharp
Until the guts of the words
Spill out
And are lost across the desk

But this is not biology!
All the same,
Frogs, mice, poems, and stories
All share one dreadful fate

A once lovely, lively frog
Is dead

A once lovely, lively poem
Is dead

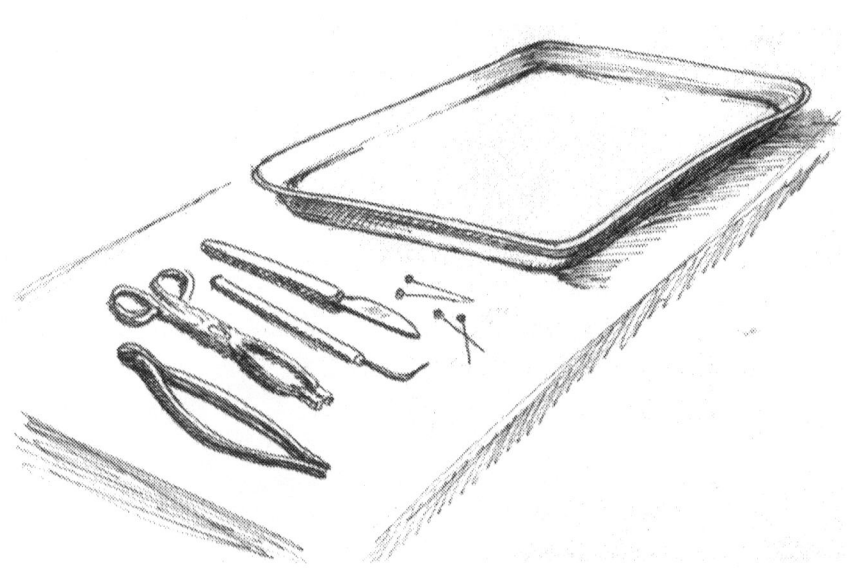

Desires

Most people despise
The cold slime from a pumpkin
But I don't
Because after
I've been waiting
In excitement for Halloween,
And for candy
And costumes
And apple cider,
A Jack O'Lantern
Is beginning

Most people despise
A hot car in the sun
But I don't
Because after
I've been caught
In a chilly wind,
A wind sucking
Every ounce of heat
From me,
A sun-warmed car
Is paradise

Most people despise
The stiffness of tent floors
But I don't
Because after
I've been imprisoned
In a classroom all week,
Staring out the window
At the lovely outdoors,
While I must do work,
A camping trip
Is freedom

Most people despise
The smell of gasoline
But I don't
Because after
I've been stuck
In a jam-packed car
On a long road trip
And I want to
Stretch my legs,
A gas station
Is relief

Most people despise
The glue taste of an envelope
But I don't
Because after
I've been busy
In my writing mode
Carefully composing
Just the right words
For a friend,
Licking the envelope
Is closure

Flight

Fly away, O Kite!
Enjoy this freedom
I give you now
Fly while you can—
For I can only bestow this liberty on you
For so long, while the wind blows strong!
And then for days or weeks
Or months at a time,
I fear you must be shut up again
In the garage or shed
For I seldom have the time
And the weather
And the longing
To send you up, up,
Up to your home in the sky
You love it now,
Swirl in your color and beauty
While you, my Kite,
Have been sent to your home

If only all knew, as you do,
My Queen of Kites,
To be free
And to fly
When told you may
And worry never
About the time spent shut up,
About the bad of past,
About the bad of future!
May all know, as you, O Kite, do
How to love and live
When given the chance

Crossing Paths

A great many stories tell tales of foreign lands. They might form cities or nations the reader will likely never visit. Sometimes, they conjure images of planets, even universes, radically different from our own.

Our story need not go that far.

Because, you see, the only world which must be imagined here is that which can fit inside a closet. Rather than draw elaborate maps and invent great countries and rivers and palaces, I need tell you only of a rack of clothes, some storage crates, and a tiny, green-and-yellow-striped rug.

This closet belonged to two people.

When one of them, Ella, first turned the knob to that closet, she was (quite understandably) under the impression that it belonged only to her. This was, after all, her first apartment after college, and she was grateful she no longer must share with a roommate.

After she wandered into the closet, intent on hanging her coat on its rack for the first time, she discovered that the previous resident had apparently left his belongings inside. A jacket, two or three sweaters, and one rain poncho were already hanging there. One pair of sandals, two pairs of sneakers, and some shiny black dress shoes sat in a neat row along the far edge. There was a mat which clearly had had feet wiped on it a few times. And near the back were some bins of gloves, hats, scarves, ball caps, water bottles, sunscreen, bug spray, a dog leash, and various other paraphernalia one takes when one goes out for a walk.

Whose is this? Ella wondered, drifting across the closet toward the bins.

Slam! The door shut behind her. Whoops. She had forgotten it was on a spring.

No matter. She would simply place a bin in front of the door to hold it open. After all, she would need it open to allow every ounce of light inside, especially since the closet's light bulb was very dim. She reached for the knob.

Suddenly, before she had yet even touched it, it swung open.

Somebody entered. A man.

"Hi, Ella!" he greeted her enthusiastically.

Ella only stared. This man looked young—more of a boy, really, within a year or so of Ella's own age. He was a tall, lanky brunette dressed in jeans and a green T-shirt. Strangely, although he most certainly was not a *large* man, Ella could not see into the room behind him.

He stepped all the way into the closet, and once again the door swung shut. Ella flinched—slightly at the noise, mostly at the realization that somehow this complete stranger and she were alone in this dark closet.

"Who are *you?*" Ella asked.

He stopped short. It was *his* turn to look frightened. "It's me... Tom..." he told her. Ella just gazed at him.

"Don't you... recognize me?" he asked her.

"No," whispered Ella. "I've never seen you before in my life."

"You haven't?" A tear materialized in his eyes. "Ever? Not even once?"

"No."

"In that case," he told her, "this must be the last time I will ever see you." He cleared his throat. "Can... will you kiss me? Just one more time?"

This guy is nuts! Ella thought, panicking. She jumped up.

"Wait!" Tom called. "Don't leave!"

As Ella raced away, Tom began to sob—the saddest, most desperate sobs Ella had ever heard. She thrust open the door and ran. Once again, it clicked shut.

The moment it did, the wailing stopped.

At least this loon didn't follow me, Ella thought. Then she began to wonder. *Sure, I have no idea* what *this guy was doing in my house. But why did he stop crying so quickly?*

Ella should have called the police. But she didn't, and if she had it wouldn't have done any good. Rather, curiosity got the better of her. She crept to the door and, opening it just a crack, peered inside using a technique similar to one she used over fifteen years ago, to inspect her closet for monsters. Now she employed it one last time.

The closet was empty.

Ella was no doubt shaken by the incident, but what could she do? She realized that the only logical explanation for this could be that she was hallucinating. Yet while Ella had never hallucinated before, she had always imagined it would feel... different. Fuzzier. Dreamier. *Drugged.*

Tom had appeared very clearly. He spoke and walked normally. He wasn't flying or changing color or sprouting strange appendages. He was a normal boy.

Seeing as there was little she could do, Ella carried herself as usual for the next couple of weeks. Wake up. Eat. Go to work. Come home. Eat. Watch TV. Go to bed. Life was normal, and the incident, disturbing as it was, nearly became forgotten.

Until her day off.

It all started when Ella arrived at the office only to discover it wasn't open. A major burglary had been committed in the same building overnight, and the police sealed the edifice until it could be determined that the place was still safe, an inspection they explained could well take at least twelve hours. Ella, not wishing to waste an hour and a half's worth of gas, decided she might as well do some shopping in a nearby mall.

Five hours later found Ella back at her closet, hanging her purchases. She strolled across the closet to retrieve a hanger which had accidentally sprung from her hands.

"Ow!"

The voice seemed to come from nowhere. Ella looked around. The door clicked behind her.

A small, curled-up figure drew himself to full height.

"T-tom?" Ella whispered. *So much for not seeing me again,* she thought.

"Hi, Ella!" Tom greeted her.

Frightened once more, Ella started to retreat, already rehearsing what to tell the police when she called them: *"Yes, this stalker keeps appearing in my house. I don't know who he is or how he got there without my noticing, but could—"*

"Are you okay, Ella?" he asked her. She nodded, because this is instinct when one asks that in so kind a tone. Tom continued.

"I brought you something." He reached into his pocket and withdrew an orange lump of tissue paper tied with white ribbon. Dazed, Ella opened it.

It was a shell.

Not just any shell, either, but one more beautiful than Ella had ever seen in her life. Its shape was similar to that of a conch, but the colors were something different. Greens, golds, and lavenders swirled around in a pool of color. It was gorgeous.

"T-thank you," Ella told him, still nervous.

"You can add it to your shell collection!" Tom exclaimed excitedly.

Ella froze. She did, in fact, collect shells. But how would Tom know that? She was positive the only time she had ever seen him was that startling incident weeks ago. "How do you know about that?" she asked. "And you know my name, and..."

Strangely, a flash of grief slipped through Tom's expression. "You've forgotten."

"Forgotten what?"

Tom coughed. "Okay, you didn't forget. You just... have nothing to remember by... yet."

"What do you mean?"

"I wish I didn't have to explain… it just means you won't remember it next time."

"Explain *what?*"

Tom sighed. "We live in opposite worlds, Ella. We live in opposite universes. And we live in opposite time."

"How can time be *opposite?*" Ella inquired.

Tom slumped down on the closet floor. "I honestly don't know. All I know is—the only way I can talk to you is through that closet. You can't get into my world. And I can't get into yours. And anything I tell you in one meeting, you forget the next. Then you never remember it again. But whenever I tell you something, it's something you've somehow known all along. It's like every meeting I can remember, you don't even know about yet, and vice versa."

He breathed, as though he were a student who had just given a lengthy answer in hopes that his teacher wouldn't notice he didn't really understand what he was talking about.

Yet Ella thought she grasped *something.* Last time, after all, Tom had said that her failure to recognize him meant he would never see her again.

It was the first Ella had seen Tom. But if time ran "opposite," it was Tom's last visit.

Her pondering resulted in awkward silence. Finally Tom said, his voice soft, "I-I'll be going now."

"Goodbye, Tom," Ella bid him kindly, hoping to make up for the cruelty she had given him last time. *You couldn't help it,* she told herself. *You thought he was some—*

The door clicked.

Ella teetered on the threshold of the closet. Finally, she slid in, feeling a nervousness and curiosity she had not known since her first dance in middle school.

She was going to wait for Tom.

She brought a novel and a flashlight (it *was* dark in the closet). She had no idea how long it would take; what were the chances of Tom popping in just when Ella happened to be there as well?

Pretty good, apparently. Just as Ella managed to get comfortable against a pile of jackets and to find her place in the novel, she heard the familiar twisting of the knob. Feeling more like Pavlov's dog than she wanted to admit, she jumped toward the door.

Sure enough, Tom stepped in.

A brief moment of uncertainty swept through Ella. What did you talk about when neither of you remembered the same things? They had nothing in common... did they?

They had a closet.

Ella stared at Tom, who stared back. Finally, he asked, "Has that light worked any better than this before?"

"No. Why?"

"Looks like I'll be left with this for the rest of my visits, then." He smiled.

Why was this so hard?

"Are... are you all right, Tom?"

He sighed. "It's just... you're forgetting so much. And I can't blame you, because I was like that... ah... several visits back..."

"What did I forget?"

"Nothing. It's trivial. It's just... I guess I'll have to explain a lot to you in these upcoming visits... won't I?"

"Yeah, you will. But what have I forgotten?"

"The... rules."

"What rules?"

"The ones that come with the closet. That is... you've been waiting for me, haven't you? Or thought you would have to wait for me." He glanced at her book.

"Yeah..."

"You didn't need to." Tom looked away and started pacing. "Think. Look at that door." Ella looked. "Is it open or shut?"

"Shut." Ella thought awhile. "And—it was when I last saw you. And the time before that." It was coming together. "And—and since I moved into this apartment, those are the only times I've been in here with the door shut—the times I've run into you." She looked him in the eye. "Why is that?"

Tom shrugged. "It's all part of the closet's magic."

"Magic? You mean... just like how both our worlds run opposite each other?"

"Sort of... but that's not part of the closet. At least, I don't think so. I think the closet's part in that sort of magic is more the fact that our worlds can even touch each other— a window. Not a doorway, mind you. We can't visit each other."

"Why not?"

"You tell me. You told me the rest of this."

51

"I did?"

"You did. Now that I think about it, you said something about me telling it to you. I guess it's like a self-fulfilling prophecy—I can tell you because you could tell me because I told you."

Tom was confusing Ella. Finally she said, "Are you sure I can't visit your world?"

He shrugged. "You seemed confidant when you told me."

Not wanting Tom to start up again, Ella grabbed his hand. "What if we were both to walk out at once?" She pulled him to the door.

"Ella, I—"

Enthusiastically, she yanked it open and stepped forward. She banged her foot.

Wincing, the girl who bruised easily looked up at what she expected to be her room or maybe Tom's.

It was a wall. The door was impassable.

Ella wheeled around toward Tom. "Let me guess—the magic."

"If it were a portal," Tom considered, "I don't think we would be able to have this conversation. Because then would the closet run on your time or mine? You would be responding to my first words with your last words, and vice versa. We would get too confused."

"I'm confused already."

"Maybe you haven't noticed—time *stops* in here. When you come out, it's the exact same time as when you entered. And that's good, because it gives us a middle ground, so one of us isn't sent back in time while we're in the other's zone or something. Haven't you noticed before?"

Ella couldn't have known. The first time she met Tom, she had been so frightened that her watch was the *last* thing she was thinking about. And the second time was a leisurely one—an unexpected day off, and checking the time would ruin the joy.

"So… I guess it's all part of the magic?"

"Yes."

"Is there anything else I should know?"

"I'll tell you other things," Tom told her, "when you stop knowing them." He put his arm gently around her. "Just know that this closet's greatest magic is something you haven't done yet, haven't known yet… but you will. Because I have."

They hugged and parted.

After that, these meetings became quite regular. Ella would shut her door, wait a few seconds, and faithful as her own heartbeat, Tom would be there. He told her things. She told him things. It didn't matter what they talked about—things were so different in each world that no matter what account one gave, the other found it fascinating.

One leisurely evening (for Ella—Tom, for all she knew, could have arrived at eight a.m. in his time), the two sat there, a single strand of Christmas lights tripling the light in the place. Ella vaguely wondered whether the electric bill would land with her or Tom, then let it go.

"Tom," she asked, "in your world, how bright is the sun? Better or worse than these lights?" She grinned feebly at the joke.

"Better," he responded, grinning back, "definitely better." He turned to Ella. "What about you? How's your sky?"

"Gorgeous," Ella breathed. "I only wish I could take you to see it. And the flowers, and mountains, and snow…"

"Snow?" Tom repeated.

"I guess you don't have it," Ella mused. "It's like cold white mush that falls from the sky. And what about beaches? Do you have them?"

"Yes," Tom answered. "Miles and miles of them. And the greatest thing about them is that the animals leave these shells—"

"Shells!" exclaimed Ella, remembering. "We have them too. I collect them…" She felt as though she had just fulfilled some prophecy.

"You do?"

He's forgotten! Of course, Tom didn't really forget. But this was the first time he didn't magically remember something without her reminding. It was a chilly feeling, and Ella's first glimpse of the inevitable.

"Yes," she whispered, getting up to leave. "I do collect shells."

Obviously, the fact that Tom had "forgotten" such a trivial detail really didn't matter so much; after all, it was a natural occurrence for two worlds sliding past each other.

But it mattered to Ella. The next time she visited Tom, and carried more conversations about their worlds and lives, it occurred to her that Tom really wouldn't remember everything she was telling him. He wouldn't be there for her forever. She had no way of telling how many visits she had left—three? Twenty? Hundreds?

Still, they were numbered for her, as they had been for Tom. Those words of his, in her very confused first visit, spoke more to her now than they had then. Now, they were the morbid words of a friend who would miss her.

Then, they were the incoherent blathering nonsense of a stranger, one who spooked her. And she ran away.

Was that what Tom would do someday?

Tom, having realized Ella's profound silence, asked, "Ella? Is everything okay?"

Ella sighed. *You have to warn him, you know. It's the next best thing you can do, other than ask for forgiveness. And how can you do that when he has no clue you've done anything?*

"I guess I... I want to say I'm sorry."

"Sorry for what?"

Sitting up straight, Ella continued. "The... first time I ever saw you... you caught me off guard. I was scared. And I... I was cruel. I abandoned you. Now I really wish I hadn't, but... I didn't know." Ella felt that was only the beginning of what she had to say, somehow. *Why?* she wondered. *You said you were sorry. Why does it matter anymore?* It mattered, though. Like what she wanted to say, very desperately, was something completely unrelated to the apology.

Finally, Tom spoke up. "I should let you know... I did the same thing. And I regret it terribly. I didn't know you yet. Still, now I... I want you to know I would never do that now."

"And I wouldn't either."

The apologies were over; now why weren't they *done?*

Something else needed saying. Tom tried to say it. "Is... is it *fair?*" he asked finally.

"Is what fair?"

"This!" He jumped. "I mean, I could have met anyone from my own world. Anyone. But somehow, it had to be *you!*" Ella flinched. Tom seemed *angry* now.

"*What* had to be me?" Ella ventured, as a fearful, knowing, yet oddly comforting tension crawled up her arm.

"If it were one from my world," Tom continued, not really hearing her, "we could have had months. Years. Our whole lives. But you—I don't have long to say I love you!"

The words had just escaped his lips when Ella realized that they would have had to. He had mentioned this before, hadn't he? Dropped hints. Had known.

Now it was Ella's turn for knowing.

She looked at Tom. Were this a boy from her own world, perhaps she would have taken his words more lightly—or more seriously? But with Tom, they were simple yet deep. They were just the course of what had to happen. Before now, Tom had remembered them and Ella hadn't. Afterward, Ella would have them and Tom wouldn't.

But now, right now, as they leaned in to kiss, they both had them. Right now. These words were theirs, to share for as long as they both could.

"I'm sorry," Tom said after a long moment. "About getting upset. It's just why can't we have more time than this? A few visits and it's over."

"Tom," Ella said slowly, "I think you need to know this: Having this time, here, with you, is worth more than the many years I will live later. It's better to be together for what we can, isn't it?"

"You're right," Tom whispered back, "It is."

And so it was.

Of course there were more visits with Tom—Ella knew from her conversations with Tom that she was guaranteed them. But they were not at all like that last visit, when this secret, this love that each had kept from the other for so long, was finally revealed to them both.

At least, though, Ella knew this much: Their love, which had grown stronger in her, was soon to grow weaker in Tom, for the ironic reason that in Tom's world his love grew stronger.

Yet it remained that, when she could and he could, they had loved. It reminded Ella of her friends when they were preteens, when they slapped high fives if they happened to pass each other on their bikes. Tom wouldn't be able to carry her for her whole journey, nor she his. But, although their lives did, in fact, run "opposite," with each just barely recognizing the other in the distance, there had been a point where they came closer... closer... and touched.

And that was where they hung on tight.

Sure enough, as much a part of the closet's rhythm as Ella's meeting Tom and their eventual love, Tom stopped remembering. And here, dutifully, she would tell him. Gradually she told him about her world, about the magic and rules of the closet, and what the closet was. And she, too, dropped hints—it was only fair, wasn't it? This, she found, was a new sort of love.

No, it wasn't the long, yet woefully short, wonderful passion she knew that one time, when Tom loved her as Ella loved him. It was the love of unreciprocated love. Tom did not love her yet. But he would have to know what she was telling him if he would ever love her. She was there so he could find out. He didn't understand it... but he would. All in good time.

She still wasn't ready for it when it hit.

She walked into the closet, listening for the familiar click of the door behind her.

Tom was already there.

"Hello, Tom," Ella greeted him.

Tom just stared. "Who are you?"

Ella's heart skipped. "You mean you don't recognize me?"

Tom shook his head.

Tears poured down Ella's cheeks. "In that case, this must be the last time I will ever see you."

The Span

It was time to go.

I can tell you very little of these two lovers as they parted. This was before my time. It was before my father's time, or his father's. It goes back to a time and place at which point I do not know my own fathers. They lived and loved long ago. And they live and love today.

One was the young woman. She was, as they call her now, of the Zuni people in an area that would one day be called the southwest. The other was the young man. He was, as they have called him always, alien, from lands we no longer know. Few know that he or his people were here. But they were. He had come and met her and her people. But now he had to go back to his people.

"I'll be back," he promised.

"When?" she whispered.

"I do not know. They say time may be different. In different places, in different worlds. I wouldn't know when I'll be back. Maybe tomorrow. Maybe in thirty years. But I will return. And before I go, I want to say I love you, Ahn." For this was her name.

"I love you, Thrin." For this was his name.

She watched him go home, all the while knowing his home was with her.

And that he would return.

And so would she.

He was going home.

Not to the home he had always called so.

To the home he had seen so many weeks ago and for which his return was much longed.

He hoped she was doing well, for he had been unable to speak with her.

He had had to speak with his planetary government about his discoveries. That had taken weeks. Six long weeks. And there was a small anomaly with his ship's propulsion system… he hoped it meant nothing. But now they were permitting him to go back. This time, there was no obligation to go to the "home" he had once loved but was now nothing to him. He loved Ahn. He was going home to see her.

The ship landed, in the very coordinates at which he and his beloved had last spoken.

It was the wrong planet. It had to be.

For nothing was the same.

It couldn't be.

Where had stood saguaros were now roads; where her adobe home had been was now a sign. It bore mysterious characters that must have been writing of some sort. But he couldn't read them.

The people were wrong, too.

They were pale, with hair that could have been dyed with the rainbow. There were all colors. Red. White. Brown. Black. Yellow. Orange. Green?

And all stared at him and his ship.

He walked away. Just walked away, in a daze. Thrin had never seen such strange people, who looked nothing like the natives he had once known.

He had walked for some time before he noticed one.

A boy, maybe five years younger than Thrin.

He did look like those he had known, like the people he had seen.

Thrin knew he must speak to him.

"These people," he breathed. "What has happened? They are not like the people who were here not long ago. How long have I been gone?"

The boy merely looked at him. "Excuse me? You actually speak Ashiwi?"

"I came to this planet not long ago. There were people here, including... including the woman I loved." Where was Ahn?

"I'm confused," said the boy in the tongue Thrin had heard just weeks ago, but now seemed so distant. "What's your name?"

"Thrin."

The boy looked at him strangely. "That's my name."

"That's odd. But please, tell me where the people went."

"What people?"

"Your people! They had to be yours. The people who lived in the adobe houses, who wore animal hides, who called themselves..." He stopped to think. "*Zuni.*"

The boy laughed. "You mean the Indians? They're long gone. My family and I are some of the last ones."

"How long have I, um … they… been gone?"

"At least two hundred years, I'm guessing."

They walked and talked.

"So where do you live?"

"A few blocks from here."

"So, uh, Thrin... how is it we have the same name?"

"I don't know where you got yours. Mine's a family tradition, legend kind of thing." His face lit up. "Maybe we're distant cousins or something!"

"But how could that be? I come from another planet." The man wasn't sure, but he thought he saw the boy's eyes lift in a strange, exasperated, upward motion.

"Anyway, I don't know exactly what the story is. I could ask my parents again. It's something about a woman whose lover left her and promised to return. Only he didn't. After many years her family forced her to marry another man. But she still missed her true lover. So she named her first son after him. So he named his first son that same name. I'm not sure what number I am."

"How many are in your family, if you don't mind my asking?"

"There's me, my parents, my sister, and my dog. Only I can't introduce you. My parents don't get home from work until seven, and they wouldn't want me to bother them at work. And my sister..." his voice trailed off. An odd, far-away look set into his eyes. "She doesn't talk. We don't know why. She was born healthy, can hear fine and has never seen any trauma. But her whole life she has never once spoken. We've tried, many times. The doctors and psychologists are all stumped. Look, that's her, coming up the sidewalk now."

The man's eyes landed on her.

He knew.

It was her, all right. It was the same eyes, the same hair. She was even standing in the strange, sad, forlorn position she had been in last time he'd seen her.

Don't ask me to explain this. Time never makes sense. Neither do words. Neither do people. Neither does love.

59

"Ahn?" he whispered.

She gaped at him.

"How did you know that was her name?" the boy asked.

"Ahn?" He took a step closer. "Ahn... do you remember me?"

Her eyes were watery, with what could have been joy, sorrow, hope, pain, or mere confusion. Her lips quivered as they parted.

"Yes."

To Natalie

A face I've never seen
Trickles through my mind
A friend I never walked with
A friend I'll never find
We could have been such merry friends
If we could meet and know
But now I've never met her--
She was taken years ago

My friend's name is Natalie
I gave her it, because
None other would have given it--
Not needed in the laws
They would not see a person
Though they knew of her existence
They took her as a youngling
Who put forth no resistance

They declared her not a human
Despite pulse and beat of heart
And in all this they justified
To pull her life apart
They read not *her* thoughts on the matter
On the life she'd hate to lose
To let this girl live life was wrong--
Was her mother's right to choose

Now I have no friend Natalie
Who's been long since swept away
Yet a question still does haunt me
And bereaves me to this day:
For children who've been life-denied
Great people have been lost
So when they take out any more,
How great might be the cost?

A Poetic Repast

Here's to that this poem
May never be required reading
Here's to that my words
May live only so long as they are wanted
And never be forced on those
Who will dread reading them
Here's to that this poem
Be a dish that is offered
To those who eagerly gobble it
But never forced upon
People who will choke on it
Here's to that this poem
May be left on the table while fresh
And taken away when cold
And spoiled
Here's to that nobody
Chokes upon undesired words
Forced, for this is as the fathers ate
Here's to that this poem's
Lovers shall pass it freely
Amongst themselves
And that it may never
Be falsely declared beloved
Here's to you,
Should you read this freely
And on your own decision
For you are the poem's lover
And to you it is still sweet
And has not gone stale

Drink up